D0978574

HERB GROWER'S GUIDE

Cooking, Spicing & Lore

John Prenis

Running Press
Philadelphia, Pennsylvania

Distributed in Canada by Van Nostrand Reinhold Ltd., Ontario

Copyright © 1974 Running Press
All Rights Reserved

Printed in the United States of America

This book may be ordered directly from Running Press.
Please add 25¢ postage.
TRY YOUR BOOKSTORE FIRST

ISBN 0-914294-07-5

Running Press
38 South Nineteenth Street, Philadelphia, Pennsylvania 19103

cover illustration
Charles Santore

interior design & illustration
Bob and Sandy Bauer

cover & package graphics
Jim Wilson

hand lettering
Werner Krupp

package design
Kevin Quinn

publication concept
Lawrence Teacher

technical advisors
Jim Dunlap, Charles Deal, and Ed Lynde

research and horticultural advisor
Otto Fridman

type setting
Alpha Publications, Inc.

cover printing
Pearl, Pressman, Liberty

DEDICATION

This book is dedicated to Dioscorides, a Greek military physician who served with the army of Nero. His short, accurate descriptions of medicinal herbs greatly influenced all herbalists who followed him.

TABLE OF CONTENTS

The symbols on this page are a compact guide to the characteristics and requirements of each herb. By looking over the symbols, you can tell at a glance which herbs are best suited to your growing conditions. More detailed information is found in the sections devoted to individual herbs.

 annual

 perennial

 height

 poor soil

 rich soil

 likes some lime

 keep well watered

 keep on the dry side

 full sun

 sun or partial shade

 shade

 won't survive frost - winter indoors

 easy for beginners

Herbs are a delight. They add a new dimension to almost any dish. Do not be intimidated by their use in esoteric and fancy cookery—herbs can add new interest to ordinary dishes as well, and you need no exotic knowledge to use them. With a pinch of herbs, routine food preparation can become creative cookery, and a commonplace meal can be turned into an adventure.

In many ways herbs are the ideal project for the beginning gardener. Herbs are not fussy about soil, they resist pests, and they will flourish over most of the United States with a minimum of care. Even a small patch of ground will yield a plentiful supply of herbs for the kitchen, and you need not even wait a full season for your harvest. All you have to do is to pinch off a few aromatic leaves whenever you need them to flavor a favorite dish. There is nothing like combining the fun of gardening with the thrill of flavoring a meal with a herb you have grown yourself.

For the purpose of this book, a herb is any plant valued for its flavor, or its fragrance. This takes in a wide variety of plants indeed, so we will concentrate on those that are especially useful, not too difficult to grow, or that have interesting stories and traditions behind them.

The discovery and first uses of herbs are lost in the far distant past. It seems most likely that discovery came about by accident, perhaps when someone walking through the brush was arrested by the pungent odor of the plant he had just trampled. It must have seemed like magic when herbs were first used with food—that such a tiny bit of leaves could cause such a wonderful change in taste. Herbs must have seemed like special friends with special powers, and it is no wonder that they quickly became tangled in myth, magic, and ritual.

Ancient civilizations used herbs not only as flavorings, but as perfumes, deodorants, fumigants, cosmetics, and medicines. Before the discovery of spices, herbs were a vital part of daily life. Egypt once exported herbs to all parts of the ancient world. At the height of their power, the Romans introduced many herbs into Britain. They grew well there, and from Britain, the Romans shipped herbs all over the Empire.

In the recession of culture that followed the Roman decline, herb lore was kept alive in the gardens of the medieval monasteries, where herbs were grown both for their medicinal value and their religious significance. Charlemagne had a large herb garden and kept records on the herbs he grew in it. The cold stone floors of monasteries and castles were strewn with fragrant herbs, and gentlemen carried nosegays of herbs to clear their nostrils of the unpleasant odors they often encountered.

The interchange between culture and the invention of printing that signaled the Renaissance encouraged the printing of many old collections of herb lore and the making of new ones. These herbals mixed accurate descriptions of plants with fantasy and folklore. Each herb was assigned a place in the zodiac. Medicines were often devised by the "doctrine of signatures" which held that a beneficent creator had provided a cure for every ill, and given every plant signs by which its virtues could be identified. A plant which attracted bees, for instance, was logically held to be good for bee stings. Extensive collections of remedies were built up, some of which are still of interest today. The word *officinale* in the name of a herb indicates that it was once used medicinally.

When the colonization of the New World began, herbs were among the first immigrants. Unable to rely on the distant homeland, settlers fell back on remedies and flavorings they could grow themselves. Many plants used by the Indians proved helpful. Every homestead had a herb garden, and carefully packed herb seeds were among the essentials carried westward by the settlers.

When improvements in transportation made imported spices widely available, the importance of herbs declined, but they carried their symbolic values well into Victorian times. Little bouquets of herbs and flowers called "tussy-mussies" were exchanged by friends. Each herb had a symbolic meaning, and a small bouquet could convey as much information as a letter.

Today many of us, accustomed to bland diets and tasteless precooked "convenience" foods, have forgotten the use of herbs. The misconception has grown that herbs are part of fancy foreign cooking, for special occasions only, and can only be used properly by professional chefs. Nothing can be further from the truth. It is easy to use herbs and to make them a part of your everyday cooking. You may never become a great cook, but if you find yourself pepping up the TV dinners with a pinch of thyme or savory, this book will have accomplished its purpose.

The Word "Herb"

How do you pronounce the word "herb" anyhow? Some people say "herb" some people say "erb", and there are always those ready to fight at the drop of an "h." Which is correct? It all depends on what dictionary you're tossing around and whether it falls heads or tails. It used to be that the word was spelled "erbe" and pronounced that way too. In those days before the invention of the printing press, however, spelling was a matter of personal taste. Somehow a silent "h" was added to the word and we've been stuck with it ever since. The "h" stayed silent until about two hundred years ago when the British began pronouncing it under the impression that dropping an "h" for any reason was Cockney, and lower class. The American colonists either never got the word or chose to ignore it. Since then, the "h"—less version has been an American affectation. Whenever an innocent pronounces the word as it is spelled, there is always a know-it-all ready to spring to his side and correct him with the "proper" pronunciation. As for myself, I pronounce the word "herb" and if anyone wants to pronounce it without the "h", he can jolly well spell it that way too.

GROWING HERBS OUTDOORS

Most people when thinking of herb gardens picture the elaborately patterned traditional sort found in botanical gardens and on large estates. The home gardener need plan nothing so complicated. A small patch of well drained soil that gets sun most of the day is all that is required. Twenty square feet of ground will grow more herb then the average family can use. Any convenient location will do, but a spot by the kitchen door has obvious advantages. When placing plants, be sure that you can reach all parts of the plot easily without stepping on anything, and make sure that the tallest plants are in the rear where they will not shade the smaller ones. Four or five plants of each kind is all you will need, unless you want to plant more to dry for the winter. That's about all there is to it.

Plenty of sun is the first essential requirement for a successful herb garden. Nearly all herbs do best with several hours of full sun each day. Some shade loving exceptions are angelica, chervil, sweet cicely, and woodruff.

Herbs are not fussy about soil. Nearly any plot of ground that will grow weeds will grow herbs. Most herbs are adapted to survival in dry rocky soil much worse than anything you will give them. What is important is *drainage*. All the herbs in this book, except where otherwise noted, require a well drained soil. Herbs simply will not prosper with water standing around their roots. A low lying spot that collects water with each rain sould be avoided when planning a herb garden. Soils that are heavy with clay should be lightened by mixing sand into them until water drains away freely.

With few exceptions, herbs will do well in ordinary garden soil without requiring much in the way of fertilizer. Fertilizer should be necessary only in crowded or long established beds where the plants have placed a heavy demand on the soil. While herbs will grow larger and lusher in rich soil, it is often said that their taste will not equal that of plants grown in poorer soil. Also worth noting is the fact that the same herb grown in different soils can vary in taste, sometimes to the

16

point where a herb grown in a foreign soil looses its distinctive taste altogether.

Herbs are not very likely to be bothered by insect pests. They are full of aromatic oils which, while appealing to us, are just too much for bugs to stomach. In fact, preparations made from herbs can sometimes be used to keep insects away from *other* plants in your garden. If you find your herbs succumbing to pests, it is quite likely they have been weakened by other causes.

In your garden you will probably have both annual and perennial herbs. Annuals, as the name implies, last only one season. As soon as they have formed their seeds, they die. Perennials, on the other hand, have roots that survive the winter, though the plants may seem quite dead above ground. Most herbs are perennials and produce new growth from the original plant each spring. Annuals must be grown afresh from seed each spring. Two common annuals are basil and dill. Some perennial herbs are grown as annuals because they are killed by cold winters, though they are perennial when given the chance.

To help perennial herbs survive the winter, it is a good idea to give them a covering of mulch. Mulch can be dead leaves, old Christmas tree branches, or any other organic refuse that is not too unsightly. The idea is to insulate the beds, not to keep them from freezing, but to make sure that once frozen they stay that way. Alternate freezing and thawing causes the soil to heave in a way that breaks plant roots and generally upsets things. Once spring has arrived to stay, you can remove the mulch and under it you will find your herbs putting out new shoots, plus very likely, many new seedlings from the seeds that were dropped last fall.

GROWING HERBS INDOORS

You can grow herbs indoors with success if you keep in mind that they are basically outdoor plants. Most homes, especially in wintertime, are too hot, too dry, and too stuffy for herbs—and sometimes for people as well. Give your herbs reasonable conditions and they will prosper—and you will probably feel more comfortable too.

The first thing to do is to lower the thermostat a couple of notches. Herbs prefer temperatures below 70°F. Don't put your herbs on a radiator or near a hot air vent. Extra humidity can be provided by putting pans of water near your plants or by putting their pots in a tray filled with pebbles and filling the tray with water to a level just below the tops of the pebbles. A window opened for a few minutes each day will give your plants fresh air, but be careful—they don't like drafts any more than you do.

If this seems like a lot of trouble to go to merely to pamper a few plants, here's another thought for you. If you carry out this program you may find yourself with an unexpected bonus—fewer colds this winter. Doctors have long claimed that our dry, overheated, stuffy homes are partly to blame for the minor illnesses we suffer each winter. Surely it makes sense to realize that when you wake up in the morning with your throat dry and raspy from breathing hot air all night, you are already on the way towards getting a sore throat.

The answer to the question of how much light you need to raise herbs indoors is simple—all you can get. Two or three hours of sun a day will suffice for many herbs, however. If you have a window that gets light but no sun, you can still grow angelica, chervil, lovage, lemon balm, mint, sweet cicely, and woodruff.

A simple basic soil mixture for herbs can be made by mixing equal parts of soil, sand and humus. The humus can be peat moss, compost, or rotted leaves. Extra fertilizer or lime can be added to the pots of the herbs that need it. Good drainage is just as important indoors, so be sure that each pot has a drainage hole. Before putting in any soil, fill the bottom quarter of each pot with pebbles or pieces of old broken pots. Keep the pots on saucers or in a tray so that the water that drains out the bottom will have a place to go.

Gardeners agree that rain water is best for plants, but lacking this, you can use tap water at room temperature. The best way to arrange this is to fill a jug with water and let it stand overnight, then refill it each day when you are through watering your plants. Check all your plants each day and water only those that need it. Most herbs should be watered whenever the surface of the soil feels dry. Give your plants a fine spray of water every day or two if you can. This helps both to wash dust off the leaves and to provide beneficial humidity. Also make it a part of your routine to give your plants a good rinse under the tap with lukewarm water each week. This not only cleans the leaves but helps to prevent insect pests from getting a foothold.

The nutrients in a pot of soil are limited. They are depleted both by the demands of the plant and by the constant passage of water through the soil. If a plant begins to show slow or stunted growth, it should be repotted in new soil or given a dose of a water soluble plant food prepared according to directions. Fertilizer should be applied with care, since it is possible to kill a plant with kindness. Do not feed a plant oftener than once a month during its growing season, and feed no more than two or three times during the winter when it is dormant.

While healthy herbs usually shrug off the attacks of pests outdoors, the less than ideal conditions indoors may weaken them to the point where they become vulnerable. A weekly washing of the entire plant, including the undersides of the leaves, is the best preventive. The idea is to wash bugs and eggs off the plant and hopefully to give pneumonia to any remaining. If an infestation does develop, a stronger treatment is to wash the plant with water to which a tablespoonful of detergent has been added. Be sure to rinse very carefully any leaves you pick for use in cooking or you may add an unintended flavor to the recipe. If your best efforts fail to get rid of the pests, it is better to throw the plant away rather than resort to sprays.

The indoor gardener is somewhat limited in his choice of plants to grow. Not only must they grow well indoors, but they should be useful or attractive enough to justify the space they take up. Herbs that are grown primarily for their seed, for instance, should be avoided because they may not get enough light indoors to flower and set seed. Some useful herbs than can be grown without too much trouble indoors are basil, chives, winter savory, mints, rosemary, thyme, sage, oregano, and parsley.

If you can follow these instructions, there is not much more you need to do for your plants. Turn them from time to time to keep them symmetrical, pick off any dead leaves, and trim back scraggly growth to keep them looking neat. With just a little attention each day, your indoor herb garden will be a source of constant enjoyment.

GROWING HERBS FROM SEEDS

There are some slow growing herbs, like rosemary and lavender, that the beginner is advised to buy as plants. There are some, like tarragon, that cannot be grown from seed at all. Most herbs, however, are easy to grow from seed, and there is no question that it is by far the least expensive and most exciting way to grow herbs.

Seed can be sown outdoors as soon as the soil warms in the spring. Clear the bed, loosen and smooth the soil, and give the bed a good soaking a couple of hours before planting the seeds. Seeds should be planted to the depth recommended on the packet. If you don't have this information, a useful rule of thumb is to plant the seeds to two or three times their width. Very fine seed is just sprinkled on the surface of the ground. When you are done, firm the soil to ensure good contact between soil and seed.

The germination times given in this book should only be considered a rough guide as to when the seeds should come up. The actual time can vary quite a bit, depending primarily on soil temperature. An unseasonable cold spell can set your seeds back a few days, and a warm spell can speed them up. Once your seeds have sprouted, you may find it necessary to shade them from the sun until they have toughened up. Water your seedlings gently with a fine spray to avoid washing them out of the ground. Do not allow them to dry out, for they will not recover.

Seeds of hardy plants can be sown in the fall, after Indian summer has passed. The cold keeps them dormant under their layer of mulch, while snow and frost soften the tough seed coats. When the soil warms in the spring, the little plants are ready to go.

When your seedlings are two or three inches tall, it is time to start thinning them out by pulling up the extra plants. This is a painful task, but it must be done to give the remaining plants room to grow. You can't possibly use all the plants from one packet of seed anyhow.

Starting herbs from seed indoors is a lot of work unless you are just growing a few plants for an indoor herb garden. Its chief advantage is that you can give your plants a head start on a short growing season. Seeds can be started in the soil mix described for growing herbs indoors. Keep the seedbed in dimness until the seeds sprout, then give them full light. Faster germination can be encouraged by putting your seedbed in a warm place, such as on top of a radiator.

You may have trouble with "damping off". This is a fungus disease which causes the seedlings to rot at the soil level. It is aggravated by too much warmth, too much dampness, and poor air circulation. Once it strikes, there is little you can do except start over. Commercially sold seed starting mixtures are sterilized to kill the organisms responsible for damping off. You can also sterilize your own soil by baking it for two hours in a 300°F oven.

The first two leaves a young seedling holds up to the light are the two "seed leaves" that were once packed with it inside the seed. They are smoothly rounded, and usually look nothing like the "true leaves" which appear later. The true leaves have the same form in miniature as those of the adult plant. When a seedling has two to four true leaves, it is ready to be transplanted from the seed bed into small pots, an operation gardeners call "pricking off". This consists of lifting the young plant gently out of the seedbed with a blunt flat instrument like a spoon handle or a tongue depressor, taking care to disturb the roots as little as possible. Then the seedling is placed in a hole previously poked in the soil with a pencil and the soil is carefully firmed around its roots. By the way, that pencil you used to poke holes in the ground has now become a "dibble."

The young plants are too delicate or 'tender' to go outdoors right away, so they must go through a process of acclimation or 'hardening off.' This means exposing them gradually to outdoor conditions while protecting them from full sun and strong winds. At the end of two weeks, they should be ready to go into the garden. Unless you have a short growing season, it is much easier to start them there in the first place.

GENERAL HINTS
ON COOKING WITH HERBS

The idea behind this book is not to give you a lot of recipes (that's what cookbooks are for) but to tell you what you need to know to use herbs creatively in your everyday cooking.

It's difficult to specify exact amounts of herbs to use for a number of reasons. The pungency of a herb varies according to the weather and soil conditions in which it was grown, and the length of time it has been sitting on your shelf. Of course your own personal taste is the most variable taste of all.

The best way to become acquainted with herbs is to buy a selection from a store. Take a bit of each and crumble it between your fingers, sniff, try a nibble. Try a little bit in a cup of broth. You will soon learn that some herbs, like chives, parsley, chervil, and summer savory are good mixers and can be used almost anywhere. Others, like basil, dill, mint, marjoram, tarragon, and thyme tend to stand out and should be mixed only with less assertive herbs. Still others, such as rosemary, sage, oregano, and winter savory are strongly pungent and should be used with caution.

In general, use twice as much of a fresh herb as dried. A longer cooking time will bring out more flavor. Be careful at first—remember you are trying for a subtle effect, not a dominating taste. If you can clearly taste the herb you added, you probably used too much. It's always easier to add more than to add less. Keep this in mind and you needn't fear spoiling anything with your experiments.

Herbs should be kept in tightly closed containers in a cool, dark place. While a shelf over the kitchen stove may be convenient, it's about the worst possible place from the standpoint of preserving the strength of your herbs. It's a good idea, by the way, to check your herbs from time to time and replace any that seem to be losing their aroma.

BASIL
Ocimum basilicum

Basil is a herb with a contradictory history. The Greeks associated it with basilisks and believed that it had the power to breed scorpions in the brain. To them, basil was a symbol of poverty and disgrace. They did not use it in cooking, but only as a strewing herb, to be trampled underfoot. Perhaps because of this, the story came about that the seed would grow only if it were cursed and trampled.

In India, on the other hand, a wild variety of basil is regarded as sacred to Krishna and Vishnu. There it is planted around homes and temples where it is believed to purify the air and ward off evil. A leaf placed over the heart of a dead Hindu is his guide into paradise.

Perhaps this helped basil overcome the poor reputation it got from the Greeks. In later times, eating basil was supposed to make the heart cheerful and merry. Women in childbirth

25

were given a leaf of basil and a swallow's feather to hold to ease their labor. And in Italy a spring of basil was worn as a love charm.

Basil is a handsome herb. It grows into a neat little bush about a foot and a half high with small bright shiny green oval leaves. It has small white flowers which start to open in July. Its scent is sweet, resembling that of a growing tomato plant. There is an ornamented purple leafed variety which is also useful in cooking.

Basil likes a well-drained humus-rich soil and sun or partial shade. It is very easy to grow from seed and will sprout in less than a week if sown when the soil has warmed in spring (it will not germinate well in cold ground). The young plants are easy to transplant and should be thinned or placed so that they are about a foot apart. Basil is an annual and must be grown from seed each year, but if your plants like the conditions you have given them, they will save you the trouble by spreading their own seeds freely.

Basil will do nicely indoors if kept pinched back and not allowed to flower. If allowed to flower and go to seed, the plant will die shortly after since it is an annual. Pinching off the tips of the branches will also help to keep the plant compact and bushy. Add a little dried cow manure to the basic soil mixture, or feed with liquid fertilizer about once a month. The soil should be kept barely moist.

Basil has a strong flavor that becomes stronger with cooking. While it has many uses, its chief fame is that it combines well with tomatoes in any form. It's also useful in meats, seafood, cheese and egg dishes, soups, stews, sauces, and poultry. Both the leaves and the flowers can be used in salads.

BAY

Laurus Nobilis

Bay leaves come from the laurel tree, a small handsome evergreen with a noble place in myth and history. The Greeks held the laurel sacred to Apollo, and called it the Daphne tree, after the nymph who became a laurel to escape the advances of Apollo. To them it was an emblem of victory, joy, and triumph. Wreaths of laurel crowned their kings and heroes. In Roman times, the scrolls that proclaimed victory were bound with laurel. It was believed that laurel trees purified the air, so when epidemics came, Roman emperors moved into the country where the laurel trees grew. If laurel trees died during a hard winter, it was considered an omen of disaster. In the time of Cicero, wedding cakes were baked on a bed of bay leaves. The Roman saying, "To look for a bay leaf in a wedding cake," gave rise to our saying, "Like looking for a needle in a haystack." The custom of crowning heroes with laurel gave us two more words. From the word for laurel berry (bacca lauri) comes the word *baccalaureate* and eventually the word *bachelor*. According to the herbalists, bay leaves soothed when added to the bath, gave strength where brewed in a potion, and kept one sober if tucked behind the ear. One herbalist went so far to say that no witch or devil, thunder or lightning, could harm a man who stood near a bay tree. Be that as it may, bay leaves were used to ornament churches well into the last century, especially at Christmas time.

It is not too likely that any readers of this book will want to try growing their own bay leaves. First, while the laurel is a small tree, it is after all a tree. Second, it is a sub-tropical plant and will not stand freezing. It can be grown outdoors in some of the southern states, but it must be grown in a tub and brought indoors in order to survive a cold winter. Those who would like to try growing a laurel tree should give it a rich soil and keep it well watered, taking care never to let it dry out. When wintered indoors, it should have a cool place in semi-shade where it will be protected from bright sunlight.

The pungent bay leaf has many uses. A single bay leaf gives a fine flavor to a soup or a stew. The leaves are also good for meats, poultry, fish, vegetables, sauces, salad dressings, and stuffings.

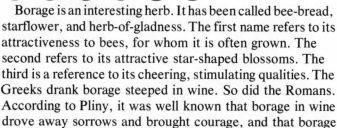

BORAGE
Borago officinalis

Borage is an interesting herb. It has been called bee-bread, starflower, and herb-of-gladness. The first name refers to its attractiveness to bees, for whom it is often grown. The second refers to its attractive star-shaped blossoms. The third is a reference to its cheering, stimulating qualities. The Greeks drank borage steeped in wine. So did the Romans. According to Pliny, it was well known that borage in wine drove away sorrows and brought courage, and that borage tea made people glad and merry. Borage became associated with courage. A stirrup cup with borage leaves floating in it was given to Crusaders leaving for the wars.

Borage is a plant with lush hairy blue-green leaves. More than anything else, it resembles a monster African violet, if you can imagine an African violet two feet tall. The star-shaped flowers appear in July and last the rest of the summer. They have a striking black center cone which is surrounded by petals that are pink when the flowers open, blue later on. Borage is an annual and must be grown from seed each year. Luckily, it is a plant which is easy to grow and requires very little care. Borage should have a rich soil and plenty of sun. The seeds should be sown where they are to grow, for borage resents transplanting. Germination time is about a week and a half. The young plants should be thinned to about a foot apart. In the fall, the mature plants will self-sow freely, insuring a new crop next year. Do not restrict borage to your herb garden. When grown among other plants, it is said to increase their resistance to pests and disease.

Indoors, borage should be given a rich soil, a cool spot, and plenty of sun. Water it often enough to keep it moist. Trim it back from time to time to keep it about a foot high—unless you plan to startle your friends by putting it among your African violets!

The leaves of borage have a pleasant cucumber flavor which makes them useful in salads. Or you can try them as pickles. Unfortunately, the leaves do not dry well. Borage leaves are good to float in cool drinks, and iced borage tea is a refreshing summer drink. Borage tea is known to have a stimulating effect on the circulation and to soothe the throat. Best of all, however is its wholesome stimulating effect.

BURNET
Sanguisorba minor

Burnet is a herb which resembles borage in both its taste and its uses. Its old greek name, "poterium" came from its use in wine cups. For many centuries burnet, like borage, was recommended for a merry heart. During the Middle Ages, burnet was one of the ingredients in a herb mixture used against the plague. Its chief medical use, however, was as an astringent to encourage the closing of wounds, and as an astringent it is still useful today.

Burnet is a perennial herb that stands about a foot and a half tall. Its leaves are deep green and fernlike with serrated edges. The purplish flowers are thimble-shaped and do not appear until the plant's second year. Burnet needs very little care. Full sun and ordinary soil are good enough for it. Burnet is easily grown from seed, which germinates in about two weeks. Since burnet grows from a tap root, it does not transplant well.

Indoors, burnet should have at least four hours of sun a day. Water it when the soil feels dry, and do not feed it, since burnet prefers a poor, dry soil. About twelve inches is a good height for burnet when grown indoors. Plants started outdoors in late summer can be moved indoors for the winter.

Burnet tastes like cucumber, so the fresh leaves can be used in salads and cold drinks just like borage. Dried leaves can be used in salad dressings and soups.

CATNIP
Nepeta cataria

Catnip is a herb that you are far more likely to find in the pet shop than at the spice counter. It was not always so, for in the 15th Century catnip was used to season soups and stews. Legend has it that chewing the roots of the plant gave one courage, while chewing the leaves made one quarrelsome. This is strange, for catnip tea is known for its soothing effects. The tea was once used to relieve colds, fever, hysteria, headaches, and nightmares. Catnip tea was a popular beverage in Europe before the introduction of Chinese tea, and it was for this use that the Pilgrims brought it to America. They introduced it to the Indians, who took to it at once. It's nice to think that after learning about so many new plants from the Indians, the settlers were able to return the favor. The principle modern use of catnip is of course, as a treat for cats, who become excited by its fragrance and dash about wildly. This is probably its oldest use too, for it seems that the Greeks and Romans knew of catnip and grew it for their pets.

Catnip is a rather untidy looking shrub that grows to a height of about three feet. The heart-shaped leaves are scalloped and covered with a velvety down. The stems are square, which immediately identifies the plant as a member of the mint family. The flowers are pink and appear from July through September. Catnip does well in a dry, sandy soil and bright sun. It is extremely hardy, surviving both drought and frigid winters. It is sometimes found growing wild near old farmhouses. As you would expect, it is easy to grow from seed. Like other perennials, it can be sown either in spring or late fall. The seeds germinate in about ten days. As long as the young plants are allowed to grow undisturbed, they are not likely to be bothered by cats, but if a leaf is bruised or broken, you will soon find every cat in the neighborhood rolling in your catnip bed. Fortunately, as the plants get older, their stems grow woody and they become far less vulverable to this sort of damage. It is worth noting that several related mints are also attractive to cats. One of these is *Nepeta mussini*. It is about a foot high and looks much neater than *N. cataria*, though it is not quite as fragrant. The common garden heliotrope, *Valeriana officinalis*, is also attractive to cats.

Catnip tea not only soothes and aids digestion, it also contains healthy amounts of vitamins A and C. To make it, simply pour a cup of boiling water over a teaspoon of the dried crumbled leaves and allow to steep for a few minutes. There are a few more things you can do with catnip. If you let your plants go to seed, you will find that birds like the seeds. The aromatic oil repels insects and some gardeners find that sprinkling plants with water in which catnip leaves have been steeped helps to keep the bugs away. It is also said that rats will not go near catnip plants, though if you consider that cats will be found wherever catnip grows, it is not hard to understand why!

CHERVIL
Anthriscus cerefolium

Chervil was a favorite of both the Greeks and Romans, who cooked the leaves like spinach and ate the roots as vegetables. It is one of the herbs that the Romans introduced to Britain. Pliny recommended it as a warming dish for cold stomachs. He also recommended vinegar in which chervil seeds had been soaked as a cure for hiccups. During the Middle Ages, chervil was said to be wholesome and charming to the spirits. It was supposed to purify the blood in the spring, and its dried leaves were used to relieve bruises and painful joints. The roots were boiled and eaten to ward off the plague. Because of its reputed rejuvenating qualities, chervil came to symbolize resurrection and new life. To this day chervil soup is eaten on Holy Thursday in parts of Europe.

Chervil is an annual that grows to a height of one or two feet. The soft golden green leaves have a ferny, lacy look somewhat like parsley. The blossoms are small and white, and they are followed by long thin black seed pods. The plant grows from a fleshy white tap root so it does not transplant well. Unlike most herbs, chervil prefers coolness and shade to bright sun. It likes a moderately rich light soil like its relative, parsley. Chervil is easy to grow from seed which should be as fresh as possible. It should be sprinkled on top of the soil, scratched in with a rake, then stamped down. The seeds germinate in about two weeks and the fast growing plants will mature in about six weeks. Thin to eight inches. Since you are interested in the leaves from the young plants, it is a good idea to make several sowings a couple of weeks apart so that you will have a continuous supply of this useful herb and plenty to dry. Pick leaves from the outside of the plant, giving the center a chance to grow.

The leaves of chervil have a delicate licorice flavor, something like tarragon. The flavor they give to food is like parsley, but more subtle. Chervil, in fact, has been called the gourmet's parsley. It blends so well with other herbs that it is almost never found alone. It is a vital ingredient of *fines herbes*, the mixture of chopped herbs used in many French dishes. Because of its amiable nature, it can be used freely almost anywhere. Some uses include salads, soups, fish, eggs, meats, vegetables, and garnishes.

CHIVES
Allium schoenprasum

Chives are a herb with a long history indeed. They were known to the Chinese two thousand years ago, who used them to control bleeding and as an antidote to poisons. The Egyptians valued chives highly and they were extensively planted in the herb gardens of the Middle Ages.

Chives look almost exactly like the wild onions that are so hard to eradicate from lawns. The thin blades grow from a mass of tiny underground bulbs. The flower is a soft purple ball that appears in early June, and it is pretty enough to earn chives a place in the garden border.

Chives are a perennial, and they are hardy even in cold climates. They need rich soil and full sun. Chives are easy to grow from seed, which germinates in about ten days. The young plants, which look like new shoots of grass, should be thinned to about six inches apart. They will eventually grow to about a foot, but it takes them a full season to reach useful size, so you may prefer to buy a pot of chives. A clump of chives can be pulled into several smaller clumps and replanted. It is a good idea to do this every couple of years to keep the plants from getting overcrowded.

Chives are easy to grow indoors. Give them plenty of sun and feed them often, especially if you cut them frequently. Chives need plenty of humidity and should never be allowed to dry out. If your chives seems to be doing poorly, make sure their pot is large enough. They may need dividing and repotting.

To harvest your chives simply cut a few blades off near the base of the clump and snip them into small bits. It is a strong grower and will quickly send up new shoots. Chives have a delicate onion flavor that does well with soups, fish, eggs, meats, vegetables, salads, and cheese dishes. Chives are rich in sulfur and, no doubt, in other minerals as well. The methods used to dry other herbs do not work well for chives. To dry chives, spread a thin layer of non-iodized salt on the bottom of a cookie sheet, spread your chives over the salt, and sprinkle another thin layer of salt to cover them. Place in a 200°F oven for ten to fifteen minutes. When done you can sift the dried chives out of the salt and crumble them into jars. Save the salt too—it is now chive salt, and can be used in the same way you use onion or garlic salt. This method can also be used to dry other herbs that are difficult to handle by conventional means.

There is a simple and delightful way to become acquainted with chives that is just too good not to give here. Chive bread is delicious, and anyone can make it. Mix some chopped chives with some soft butter and spread the mixture on slices of the best bread you can buy or make. Then reassemble the slices into a loaf, tie together, and bake for twenty minutes in a 350°F oven. Serve at once.

GARDEN CRESS or CURLY CRESS ™
Lepidium sativum

This member of the mustard family has a pungent taste
resembling that of its relative water cress. Garden cress,
however, is much easier to grow. It is grown primarily as a
salad plant, though the roots are sometimes used as a
condiment. In Abyssinia, the seeds are pressed to obtain an
edible mustard flavored oil. Cress is a source of vitamin C
and was once used in medicine to prevent scurvy and to
cleanse the blood. Garden cress is believed to be a native of
Western Asia or North Africa. Today it is found growing wild
in many parts of Europe and North America where it has
escaped from gardens.

Cress is an annual with leaves resembling those of parsley.
Left alone, it grows from eight to sixteen inches tall. It is a

™W. Atlee Burpee Co.

fast grower—some of its close relatives are troublesome weeds. In June it puts forth small white flowers which are followed by small oval seed pods in the fall. The best thing about garden cress is that it is very easy to grow and is ready to use in about two weeks, since it is eaten in the seedling stage. Indoors, cress does not even need soil. The seed is sprinkled on anything that is soft and absorbs water—a pan lined with cotton or a piece of carpet or even an old fiber doormat. Then the seeds are thoroughly soaked and covered with a piece of wax paper for two days. When the seeds have sprouted, the wax paper can be removed and the pan placed in a window. Garden cress does not need bright sunlight. The seedlings should be kept moist until they are about two inches tall and ready to cut and use. By planting new batches of seed every two weeks, you can have fresh young cress all winter. To grow garden cress outdoors, simply sprinkle the seed over the earth and cover lightly with fine soil. Keep the bed moist by gently watering with a fine spray daily until the cress is tall enough to use.

The smell and peppery taste of garden cress leave no doubt that it is a member of the mustard family. In fact, one of its wild relatives in known as "peppergrass." The tangy sprouts are excellent in salads and sandwiches and make an attractive garnish. And some cress each day keeps scurvy away.

DILL
Anethum graveolens

Dill has been known for a long time. An Egyptian medical papyrus from 3000 b.c. mentions it. Some scholars think that dill may have been the "anise" of scripture. It is not necessary to describe the flavor of dill to anyone who has ever enjoyed dill pickles. That taste has long been known to stimulate the appetite and the digestion. Similarly, the smell of dill is said to arouse the brain and fire the will, and to overcome the depressing effects of fatigue and stale air. The Greeks and Romans used it in this way, for they burned it as incense and hung wreaths of it to freshen the air in their kitchens and banquet halls. The name "dill", however, comes from the Norse *dilla*, which means "to lull." Dill tea has a mild sedative effect on the nervous system and was once used to soothe babies. Apparently dill was thought to have a soothing effect on the upper air as well, for it was once burned to drive away thunderstorms. Dill was once used to cast spells and to make protective charms against witchcraft. Part of a seventeenth century poem goes,

"There with her Vervain and her Dill
That hindreth witches of their will."

One more use of dill: brides used to put it in their shoes with a sprinkling of salt for good luck.

Dill is an upright, branching plant with blue-green feathery foliage. It grows to a height of two or three feet. The flowers are yellow and lacy, somewhat like Queen Anne's lace. When it blooms, the plant is practically all stem and flower, so those who want a continuous supply of the foliage are advised to plant several batches a few weeks apart. Dill is an annual and very easy to grow from seed. It likes plenty of sun and a rich soil. Sow the seed on top of the soil and stamp down. The germination time is about a week and a half, and the young plants should be thinned to about six inches apart. Dill is one of the herbs that does not transplant well. The young plants mature quickly, in about six weeks, and will drop seeds for the next crop if you let them alone long enough.

Growing dill indoors is not difficult if you can give it plenty of light and at least four hours of direct sun daily. Keep the plants slightly moist. Indoors, dill grows about a foot high. If plants started outdoors are brought in in the fall, you can keep them through the winter.

The entire dill plant is aromatic, so stalks, leaves, flowers, and seeds can be used in cooking. The seeds are seeds and everything else is "weed." Dill seed is somewhat stronger than dill weed. Dill weed is good for flavoring fish, potatoes, and peas, salads, sauces, meats, and vinegar. The seeds are good in bread and bean soup and, of course, pickles.

GERANIUMS
Perlargonium

The geranium is a popular plant, widely grown for its pretty flowers. The geraniums discussed here, however, are grown for their scented leaves and not their flowers, which are hardly worth noticing. There are over fifty varieties of scented geranium, and their soft hairy leaves smell of practically every aromatic substance you can think of, from pine to nutmeg. They originally came from the Cape of Good Hope, where some of them grow as tall as trees. Some popular ones are *Perlargonium graveolens* (rose), *P. limoneum* or *crispum* (lemon), *P. tomentosum* (peppermint).

Geraniums are hardy perennials and easy for the beginner to grow. They like a spot with rich loamy soil and sun or partial shade. The seeds can be planted in the spring or late fall and will germinate in three weeks or a little longer, depending on the variety.

43

Indoors, geraniums like it cool, 70°F or less. They should have two to four hours of sun a day. They need a rich, well drained soil and should be fed about once a month. Geraniums should be watered thoroughly and then allowed to dry out before the next watering, though not so much that they wilt. Trim them from time to time to keep them shapely. The cuttings can be used to grow new plants. Take a stalk at least four inches long, and put the bottom two inches into a mixture of sand and soil. Put it in a shady place, water it, and in a few weeks it should perk up and start to put out new leaves. When this happens, it can be potted and given its own place on the window sill. If the cutting does not root immediately, have patience. Some varieties take up to three months to root.

While the main reason for growing scented geraniums is so you can crush an occasional leaf between your fingers for the lovely fragnance, they have a few culinary uses as well. The leaves can be used as a garnish for fruit dishes and salads. Put a few rose geranium leaves in your sugar bowl—the sugar will absorb the fragrance and make a very pleasant addition to your morning cereal. And a few rose geranium leaves give a wonderful lift to a batch of home made apple jelly.

LAVENDER
Lavendula officinalis or *vera*

It is not too likely that you will be finding any cooking recipes involving lavender, for this herb is grown exclusively for its wonderful fragrance. Yet it was used in the seventeenth century to flavor not only confections, but all sorts of food. It may be that we are missing something.

Lavender has a long history of use. It was loved by all the ancient people, who used it extensively in their sacrifices and as a strewing herb. The dried blossoms brought a good price in the marketplace. The Greeks and Romans used it in their baths to soak away stiffness and weariness. Curiously, lavender is one herb they did not use in their wreaths and garlands—for some reason it was associated with snakes.

The smell of lavender makes you think of freshness and cleanliness, and this has always been one of its primary associations. During the Middle Ages, lavender became associated with Mary and represented purity and virtue. It's freshening qualities gave it its name, which comes from the latin "to wash." For the time in England, a washer woman was also called a lavender. Both Arab and English physicians believed the herb to have antiseptic properties. Lavender water was once used as a mouthwash. Perhaps the ultimate expression of faith in its purifying abilities was its burning in great bonfires on St. John's Eve to drive away evil spirits.

The other traditional association of lavender is with the head and the nervous system. Smelling lavender is an old remedy for headaches and jumpy nerves. According to the herbalists, a cap of lavender flowers would comfort the brain and relieve diseases of the head. Farmers once wore lavender on their hats to prevent sunstroke. Just to look on growing lavender was supposed to inspire joy and dispel sadness. Lavender has been used to stimulate the nerves and the appetite and to relieve aches and rheumatism. In the seventeenth and eighteenth centuries, young ladies who felt faint were often revived with lavender salts. Today, lavender is listed as a stimulant for the relief of hysteria, faintness, and headaches.

Lavender is a low shrub, about two feet high, with narrow velvety gray-green leaves. The small flowers are lavender (of course!) and appear in June in close spikes. Lavender is a perennial, and quite hardy. It will survive cold down to 0°F if protected with mulch. Like other herbs, lavender needs sun and well drained soil. It prefers a sweeter soil than most herbs, so give it a little lime. Lavender can be propagated from seed, cutting, or root divisions. The last two are probably better for the beginner, for lavender needs a long germination period in cold soil. The seeds should be sown in early spring or late fall and covered thinly if at all. The seedlings grow very slowly, reaching only two or three inches the first season, and do not reach a useful size until the second season.

Indoors, lavender needs at least four hours of sun daily, and a temperature range of 40-70°F. Add a little fertilizer and lime to its soil, and keep it moist at all times. Repot the plants every year, using fresh soil.

Lavender is very easy to dry. You can use it for sachets to keep your linen smelling fresh, or brighten your bath with it. Or you can try making lavender sugar by putting a few stalks and some sugar in a small jar.

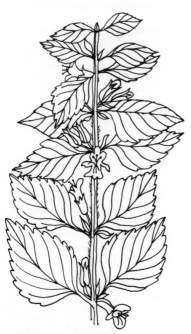

LEMON BALM
Melissa officinalis

The leaves of lemon balm have a delightful lemony fragrance. According to an Arab proverb, this herb makes the heart merry and joyful. From the days of the ancient Greeks down to Victorian times, it was supposed to benefit the nervous system, strengthen memory, and chase melancholy. According to the ancients, it could only be picked without mishap if music was played to distract the snakes which always guarded it. Serpents aside, anyone who picks lemon balm usually faces stiff competition from the bees that swarm around its flowers. It has been called the Bee Herb, and its Greek name, *melissa* means 'honeybee'. Beekeepers once used it to attract swarms to new hives. Because of its attractiveness to bees, the crushed leaves were used to soothe bee stings. Greek physicians used it to close battle wounds. According to Pliny, the bleeding would be stopped just as well if the herb were applied to the weapon that had caused the wound! The plant was also a popular strewing herb, and was one of the herbs that the Romans took to Britain. At one time it was believed that an entire dried plant sewn into an amulet and worn by a woman under her dress would make her agreeable and loved by all she met.

An English herbal recommended balm tea for students to drive away heaviness of mind, sharpen understanding, and increase memory for exams. Today we know that lemon balm does have good effects on digestion and circulation, and that its oil is indeed effective in dressing wounds.

Lemon balm closely resembles mint in many ways. It is a hardy perennial that grows to a height of about two feet. The leaves are thin and heart-shaped with deep veining. The square stems tell you at once that this plant is a member of the large and numerous mint family. The flower buds are yellow but turn white as they open. Lemon balm does well in fairly rich, moist soil with sunlight or partial shade. In fact, it may do too well, for like other mints it has the habit of spreading like a weed. It grows well from seeds. Sow them in early spring, and then be patient, for it may take them over a month to germinate. Once up, however, the seedlings grow rapidly. Trim the plants often to keep them within bounds. Lemon balm can also be propagated by cutting and by root division. Simply dig up a clump in early spring, cut it apart with the shovel, and replant the pieces you want to keep.

Indoors, give lemon balm a rich soil and two or three hours of sun a day. Like the other mints, it likes moist soil and can even be grown in a pot without drainage holes. As it grows, pinch back the tops to encourage busy compact growth.

In the kitchen, lemon balm is useful wherever you need the taste of lemon. Use it sparingly in mint sauce, with fish, lamb, beef, in salads, and fruit dishes. A crushed leaf left in a cold drink or a glass of iced tea for a few minutes will give it a fine lemon flavor.

LEMON VERBENA
Lippia citriodora

Here is another herb that is actually a tree. Lemon verbena comes from the mountainous part of Central and South America, where, unpruned it reaches a height of ten feet. The whole plant smells of lemons. The conquistadors who discovered it took specimens to Spain, whence it spread over Europe. In Latin America it has the name "herba luisa" and is used in healing.

Lemon verbena is hardy only south of Virginia. Elsewhere it is strictly an indoor plant. It requires sun, a rich soil and frequent feedings during its growing period. Keep it well watered. If grown in a tub, it can be placed outdoors in summer and brought indoors before frost—when it will show its resentment at the change in climate by dropping its leaves. The plant should be pruned regularly to keep it to a reasonable height and washed weekly to keep it free of pests.

Young cuttings root well, but the person who wants to grow this plant will probably have to buy one from a nursery.

The long lemon-scented leaves of lemon verbena can be used wherever a lemon flavor is needed—stuffings, poultry, fish, desserts, fruit drinks and preserves. It makes a nice tea, and can sometimes be used in place of mint. The main reason for growing lemon verbena, however, is for its fine lemony fragrance.

LOVAGE
Levisticum officinale

Lovage is another herb from the Mediterranean. The Greeks and Romans grew it as a medicinal herb. It also grew in the herb gardens of Charlemagne and in the medieval monasteries. Herbalists recommended it as a cure for red eyes and freckles, and as a gargle and mouthwash. Modern users are more likely to be interested in its taste, which resembles celery with a touch of curry.

Lovage is not a herb for the small garden. This hardy perennial can grow six or eight feet tall. Lovage can be used as a background plant that is both attractive and useful. The smooth dark green leaves are deeply cut and almost fernlike. In June blossom stalks shoot up to five feet to bear small yellow flowers and later, aromatic seeds that are liked by birds. Lovage is not difficult to grow and needs little care. Seed should be started in the fall as soon as it is available. In the spring the young plants can be set out where they will have a rich soil and plenty of sun. Space about two feet apart. In hot climates lovage may need shade part of the day. Lovage makes strong deep roots. In the fall a plant that is two or three years old can be dug up and the roots divided to make more plants. Indoor, lovage can be dwarfed in a pot to a size of twelve to fifteen inches. It will grow in shady windows, but does much better with direct sunlight.

The seeds, stalks, roots, and leaves of lovage are all flavorful. The fresh leaves can be used wherever the flavor of celery is wanted. Soups, stews, chowders, salads, and meat loaf are good places for fresh lovage. It should be used sparingly, however, because the taste is stronger and harsher than cultivated celery. One leaf of lovage, for instance, will flavor enough soup for three or four people. Dried lovage is good in sauces and poultry dressing. Lovage seeds can be used in cakes and breads. Even the hollow stems are useful—they make fine drinking straws!

MARJORAM
Origanum majorana or *Origanum hortensis*

This herb was a great favorite of the Greeks and Romans, who found it growing freely in the high meadows and hills around the mediterranean. The Greeks gave it a name meaning 'joy on the mountains.' They used it in food, perfume, medicine and as a strewing herb. Both Greeks and Romans used garlands of it to crown your lovers, so marjoram came to be symbolic of happiness—and blushes! It was also held to ease grief, so it was often planted on graves for the peace of the soul. A good growth of marjoram on a grave meant the soul of the person there was at rest. In later times, herbalists recommended that people carry some marjoram around with them and sniff it often to preserve health. Before the introduction of hops, marjoram was used to flavor ale. And dairymen laid springs of marjoram and thyme beside new milk to keep it from curdling during a thunderstorm.

Marjoram is a small erect bushy plant with velvety gray-green oval leaves. It grows about a foot tall. The flowers are tiny white tubes which appear in knot-like clumps. Marjoram is a perennial, but it can only survive the winter where there is no frost. Farther north, it must be grown afresh from seed each year, like an annual. Marjoram likes a sunny spot with sweet soil. It is an easy plant to grow from seed. Sow in warm weather and cover very lightly. The seeds will germinate in ten to twelve days. Thin to about eight inches apart. Marjoram can also be propagated by dividing a clump of mature plants, and by rooting cuttings. It's a good herb to dry for the winter.

Indoors, marjoram likes sun and warmth and an extra teaspoon of lime in its soil. Water it often enough to keep the soil barely moist, and keep it pinched back to a compact height of eight inches or so. A weekly wash with warm water helps to keep the leaves free of dust and insects.

Marjoram has a warm pleasing taste that, while delicate, is surprisingly pervasive. It sort of spreads and blends things. Herbs it blends especially well with are basil, thyme, chives, and parsley. Marjoram is a very useful and versatile herb. You'll find it called for in meats, fish, poultry, soups, stews, salads, vegetables, egg, macaroni and cheese dishes, sausage, and stuffings. In other words, almost everywhere.

MINTS
Mentha

The fresh cool taste of mint has made it a favorite through the centuries. To the Greeks, the smell of mint meant strength, and they used it extensively in their ceremonies and to perfume their baths. Athletes scented their bodies with it. The Athenians, who used many herbs for that purpose, went so far as to reserve mint for rubbing on their weapons to give them extra strength in battle. In Biblical times, mint was so valued that the Pharisees could pay their tithes with it. The Romans used mint by the bale. They strewed it on floors and rubbed tables with it, put it in their baths, and ate it to comfort and strengthen the nerves. And they invented mint sauce. Mint was one of the herbs the Romans grew in Britain. It seems to have fallen out of use with the decay of the Empire, however, for the Crusaders discovered mint all over again and brought it back to Europe. Mint was an important plant in the herb gardens of the medieval monasteries. Its essence was used to clear the head and quicken the senses. It was used as a hairwash and rubbed on teeth to whiten them. (Did you think mint toothpaste was something new?) In feudal Japan, officials carried mint in little silver boxes hung from their belts. Irish physicians recommended that mint be put in food and drink for merriment, but cautioned that it be used sparingly, for death could result from too much merriment!

The mints form a large family that includes many other herbs. The scents available include not only mint, but apple, lemon, and pineapple, plus many variations. The members of the family all have in common a love of moist shady places with rich soil. Unlike other herbs, which demand good drainage, mints seem to like having their feet wet. Another badge of the mint family is their square stems, by which you can tell them anywhere. Mints are also notorious for their creeping roots, which spread in all directions to form a dense mat which will eventually crowd everything else out of the bed. Because of this, mints should be grown in tubs or in separate beds edged with brick or metal sheeting. It's a good idea to lift and divide mints or move them to new beds every two years to prevent overcrowding. Mints are strong growers and should be kept well fertilized. Do not use manure for this, since it can carry spores of a bad rust disease. Mint can be grown from seed, but it is so much easier to grow it from root divisions that it is scarcely worth the trouble. Anyone with a bed of mint is usually happy to give clumps of it away to friends, neighbors, or perfect strangers. For those who would like to try, however, the germination time is about two weeks and the young plants should be thinned to about twelve inches apart.

There are many varieties of mint. Some of the most popular are listed below:

Mentha spicata - This is the most commonly grown kind, and the one usually called spearmint. It has smooth bright green leaves that are narrow, pointed and sharply toothed at the edges. It grows to two or three feet and has a rather sprawling form.

Mentha crispa - This is another spearmint - flavored variety.

57

Its heart shaped crinkled leaves make it attractive as a garnish.

Mentha piperita - This is the mint with the strongest peppermint taste. A tea made from it is a traditional remedy for stomach upsets.

Mentha rotundifolia - This mint has an apple fragrance. The leaves are soft and round with a down that has given it the name of ''woolly mint''. It is a tall sturdy plant that needs less water than most mints.

Mentha varigata - A pineapple fragrance distinguishes this mint. The leaves are marked with white, making it one of the prettiest mints.

Mentha citrata - This mint has an orange fragrance that seems to intensify the scents of other herbs growing nearby. The young leaves are heart shaped and edged with purple.

When mixing soil to grow mints indoors, use less sand and more organic material. The plants should have two or three hours of sun a day and should be turned often. Mints, unlike most herbs, can be grown in a container that has no drain holes. Water them often, but don't overdo it. Trim the plants back frequently to keep them at a height of eight or ten inches.

Mint is high in vitamins A and C and has been helpful in curing scurvy and preventing night blindness. The fresh leaves are used in salads, desserts, and garnishes. Mint makes mint sauce for lamb or fish. There's mint jelly and mint vinegar. A little mint improves pea soup. Mint adds a refreshing taste to cold drinks, and of course, there's always the famous mint julip.

OREGANO (Or pot marjoram)
Origanum vulgare

The situation in regard to oregano is somewhat confusing. The flavor, a somewhat more pungent version of marjoram, is shaded by several plants, some of which are not even closely related. As a result, botanists, not to mention seed catalogs, cannot agree on what should be called oregano. "Real" oregano, the kind you buy at the store, is imported from Greece. It is not grown in the U.S. because the plant is not hardy here. If you live in a warm part of the country, however, you might try planting some seeds from a jar of store bought oregano and seeing what comes up. The plant named here (origanum vulgare) is what most seed catalogs offer as oregano. It does not quite have the flavor of 'real' oregano, but it will do for most purposes, and it will grow in all but the northern parts of the U.S.

Origanum vulgare is a perennial that grows to a height of

59

about two feet. Its dark green oval leaves are smooth on top and woolly underneath. The blossoms which can be white, pale lavender, or dark pink, appear in August and September. The plant is related to the mints and like them it has spreading roots which will take over a whole bed if you let it. It likes full sun but will grow practically anywhere. *O. vulgare* is easy to grow from seed. Sow the fine seed in the early spring. Press it in, but do not cover. It takes three weeks or more to germinate. The young plants should be thinned to about twelve inches apart. Established plants will self-seed freely. Propagation can also be accomplished by means of root division—in fact, mature plants need to be lifted and divided every few years to prevent overcrowding. When grown indoors, *O. vulgare* should be given the same treatment as marjoram.

The name *Origanum*, which forms part of the name of a large group of plants, comes from Greek words meaning 'ornament of the hills.' It grows wild there, and the meat of the goats that feed on it becomes delicately flavored by the herb. While widely used in Greece and Italy, Oregano was little known here until ufter W.W. II. Now it is well known as an essential ingredient in pizza, and many other Italian dishes. The flavor of oregano is somewhat like marjoram, but stronger and with minty overtones. *Oreganum vulgare* seems weaker and mintier when compared with Grecian oregano. Both are useful with meats, poultry, soups, sauces, gravies, salads, fish, and shellfish.

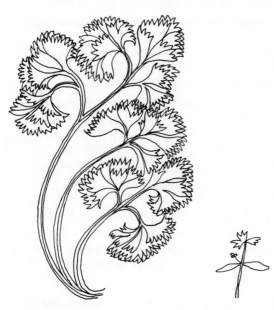

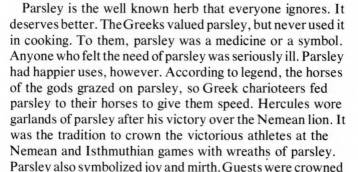

PARSLEY

Petroselinum crispum and *Petroselinum hortense*

Parsley is the well known herb that everyone ignores. It deserves better. The Greeks valued parsley, but never used it in cooking. To them, parsley was a medicine or a symbol. Anyone who felt the need of parsley was seriously ill. Parsley had happier uses, however. According to legend, the horses of the gods grazed on parsley, so Greek charioteers fed parsley to their horses to give them speed. Hercules wore garlands of parsley after his victory over the Nemean lion. It was the tradition to crown the victorious athletes at the Nemean and Isthmuthian games with wreaths of parsley. Parsley also symbolized joy and mirth. Guests were crowned with it to give them tranquility and good appetite. Finally, parsley was placed on tombs, where it came to signify oblivion.

Parsley was one of the herbs the Romans grew in Britain

for export to the rest of the Empire. To them, parsley symbolized festivity. Wreaths of it were worn during banquets to prevent drunkeness. Parsley was also supplied between courses and chewed to cleanse the breath of garlic and onion, a trick that works just as well today. From this practice comes our traditional use of parsley as a garnish.

Parsley was one of the herbs grown by Charlemagne. A cheese flavored with parsley seeds was a special favorite of his, and he ordered two cases of it a year. Parsley seed was also said to prevent baldness if rubbed on the head three times a year. The slow germination of parsley irritated many people, who had a ready explanation: before it could sprout, parsley had to go to the Devil and back nine times. Since he liked it as much as anyone else, he kept a little of it each time, which is why it appeared so spottily when it did finally come up! Perhaps because of this, parsley was supposed to be planted on Good Friday to insure a good harvest, preferably by a pregnant woman.

Parsley is part of a large family of plants grown mostly for their spicy seeds - dill, caraway, cumin, coriander, chervil, anise, fennel, lovage, sweet cicely. Parsley is a biennial, meaning that it takes two full seasons to reach its full growth and produce its seeds. Since it is the leaves that are of interest, most people treat it as an annual. *Petroselinum crispum* is the common curly-leafed parsley familiar to everyone. *P. hortense*, or Italian parsley, has larger flatter leaves along with a stronger taste and more food value. Parsley is not difficult to grow. It likes a rich soil, sun or partial shade, and plenty of water, especially when young. The seeds should be sown early to give them plenty of time to germinate. A preliminary overnight soaking helps. If you decide to transplant some of the plants to raise indoors, do it before they get very large. Parsley grows from a thick fibrous taproot and resents transplanting. Some old gardeners hold that it's bad luck to transplant parsley. It may not be bad luck for you, but it's certainly bad luck for the parsley! Thin the young plants to about eight inches apart and they will grow to a foot at the end of their first season.

Indoors, give parsley soil that is enriched with a little dried cow manure. Give it a pot with plenty of room for its long tap root (up to 10 inches long) and put it in a cool spot well away from stoves or radiators. Give it sun and keep it moist. Cut the outside leaves for use, keeping the plant about ten inches tall. Since parsley is a biennial, it's a good idea to start new plants each year.

There is an interesting trick you can use that will give you fresh parsley all winter long. In the fall, dig up the roots of some parsley plants and replant the largest ones indoors in pots of sand. Water them occasionally and the roots, using the reserve of food stored during the summer, will continue to send up new green shoots for the rest of the winter. When spring comes, you can discard them and start new plants from seed.

Recent studies have shown that parsley is an excellent source of vitamins A and C as well as iron. The flat leafed variety has more vitamin C and dries better than the curly. Parsley is one of the few herbs that keeps its flavor and its food value when oven dried. To do this spread the leaves on a tray in a thin layer and dry in a 400°F oven for five minutes. Turn them over halfway through. The crisp leaves can be crumbled through a course screen and stored in a tightly closed jar. Both fresh and dried leaves can be used with meats, fish, poultry, soups, salads, casseroles, omelets, sauces, creamed vegetables, stews, and eggs. And of course the fresh leaves are always useful as a garnish. The next time you find parsley on your plate, don't leave it there—eat it!

ROSEMARY
Rosmarinus officinalis

    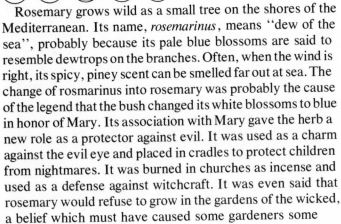

Rosemary grows wild as a small tree on the shores of the Mediterranean. Its name, *rosemarinus*, means "dew of the sea", probably because its pale blue blossoms are said to resemble dewtrops on the branches. Often, when the wind is right, its spicy, piney scent can be smelled far out at sea. The change of rosmarinus into rosemary was probably the cause of the legend that the bush changed its white blossoms to blue in honor of Mary. Its association with Mary gave the herb a new role as a protector against evil. It was used as a charm against the evil eye and placed in cradles to protect children from nightmares. It was burned in churches as incense and used as a defense against witchcraft. It was even said that rosemary would refuse to grow in the gardens of the wicked, a belief which must have caused some gardeners some anxious moments.

Thanks to Shakespeare, everyone knows that rosemary is for remembrance. It was once thrown into open graves as a tribute to the memory of the departed. Rosemary was also credited with the ability to strengthen the memories of the living. Using a comb made of rosemary wood was supposed to keep you clear headed. Greek students once twined rosemary in their hair while studying for exams to keep their minds active.

Rosemary is also a symbol of friendship, faithfulness, and loyalty. Rosemary was once an important part of weddings. It formed part of the bridal wreath, was given to the guests, and was carried by the bride from her old home to the new. Once there, she was expected to grow it in her kitchen garden, for rosemary was said to thrive wherever the woman was dominant.

Greek and Roman physicians used rosemary for many ailments. It was believed that a bag of rosemary leaves in the bathwater would strengthen the sinews. In medieval times, rosemary was a popular strewing herb, and its wood was used to make lutes. Herbalists esteemed it as a cure for nervous headaches. The Elizabethans used it both for beautifying the hair and for preventing baldness. Rosemary is an ingredient of some hair oils today. With its many uses, it is no wonder that rosemary is also reputed to bring good luck.

Rosemary is an upright shrubby perennial. It can grow to three feet or more and looks very much like a miniature fir tree. Its leaves are smooth dark green needles. Rosemary likes sun and a soil sweetened with a little lime. It can be grown both from seeds and cuttings. The seeds take about three weeks to germinate, and the growth of the plants is slow. Rosemary is not for the impatient grower. It grows about half a foot per season, so it really isn't big enough to use until its second year. Rosemary should always be kept well watered. If your area has cold winters, be prepared to take your plants inside, since rosemary is not hardy below 15°F.

Rosemary can be grown indoors with less light then many herbs. Give it a little lime in its soil and feed it regularly. It should be kept moist and misted often. If allowed to dry out, the plant will die. Rosemary should also be kept cool - about 55-60°F. It will drop its needles if it gets too hot. Rosemary should be planted in a smallish pot, since it will bloom more often if it feels slightly crowded. Turn it frequently to keep it green on all sides.

Most meats and poultry taste better with rosemary. It is also good in soups, stuffings, sauces, salad dressings, and vegetables, and it is especially recommended for baking powder bisquits. White wine that has had rosemary steeped in it for a few days stimulates the brain and nervous system, and rosemary tea is supposed to clear your head when you suffer from a cold.

SAGE
Salvia officinalis

Today sage is familiar as an essential ingredient in the stuffing without which no holiday turkey is complete. To the ancients, sage was a miracle drug. It was used for almost everything, but most important of all, it was believed to prevent the decay of age and preserve the vigor of youth. An old Latin proverb goes, "How shall a man die who has sage in his garden?" Sage was supposed to quicken the senses, clear the mind, strengthen the memory, and improve the sight. It was held to renew the sinews, turn gray hair to black, and to generally reverse the ravages of age. The name *Salvia* comes from the Latin for healthy or well. In the Middle Ages, sage was called *Salvia Salvatrix*, which shows you how highly it was regarded. Sage was used for rheumatism, sore throats, ulcers, and tuberculosis. Sage steeped in wine was used as a mouthwash, and sage tea prevented colds. This last has the support of modern science, for sage is a source of vitamins A and C. Sage makes a very acceptable tea and was widely drunk by Americans during the embargo when British tea was unavailable. Sage tea was prefered in China, where some Dutch traders made their fortunes by trading sage for Chinese tea—at the rate of four bales of Chinese tea for one of sage! Sage tea is a favorite in China to this day. More prosaically, sage was early discovered to be a digestive—that is, it aids in the digestion of fats. It became customary to garnish roast duck or goose with a sprig of sage for diners to nibble on. Then the great day came when some one got the idea of cooking the sage along with the fowl—and invented stuffing!

Sage is a neat shrubby plant with many branches. The leaves are broad and deeply veined with a pebbly surface. They are a distinctive shade of gray green - sage green, in fact. The stems of sage are square, which identifies it as still another member of the mint family. Sage is a perennial that keeps its leaves in the coldest of winters. It will survive winters as cold as −20°F. In the early spring it brings forth showy spikes of bluish-lavender flowers that are loved by bees.

Sage is an easy plant to grow from seeds or cuttings. Still another way is to bury the end of a branch and let it root to form a small plant that can be eventually cut away from the parent. Sage likes a warm dry sunny spot. Seed can be sown in early spring and will germinate in three to four weeks—sooner if the soil is warm. The young plants should be thinned to about a foot apart. They will eventually grow to about two feet tall. Divide in fall and replant every 3-4 years.

Indoors, give sage sun and a little lime in its soil. Water thoroughly and allow the surface of the soil to dry before watering again. Wash the leaves from time to time, and feed about once a month. Keep the plant pinched back to keep it bushy and about a foot high.

The leaves of sage have a sharp, peppery taste. Sage is one of the strong herbs and should be used sparingly. Just a little combined with some marjoram and thyme adds the proper taste to stuffings. Sage is also good for sausage, soups, sauces, dressings, and cheese dishes. Don't forget to try sage tea. It may not keep you young forever, but if it keeps the sniffles away this winter, isn't that enough?

SUMMER SAVORY
Satureja hortensis

Summer savory is another of the many herbs native to the Mediterranean region. The prancing satyrs wore wreaths of it. The Greeks and the Romans blended it with thyme for soups and stuffings and used it in their fish and meat sauces. The Romans took it to Britain with them, and it was one of the herbs grown in Charlemagne's herb gardens. It got the name of summer savory because its flavor was best when picked in the early summer. The crushed leaves of summer savory have been used since ancient times as a remedy for bee and wasp stings and are still good for this purpose today. According to one herbalist, savory protects against "blastings by planets, gunpowder, and lightning." Dieters should be interested in this herb - it was once eaten by fat people in the belief that it would help them grow thin.

Summer savory is a slender branching plant with narrow

leaves on firm stems. The flowers look like small pink raindrops and are very attractive to bees. In the late summer, the leaves turn a purplish brown. Summer savory is an annual, which means that you will have to grow it fresh from seed each year. Fortunately, savory is an easy plant to grow. The seeds should be sprinkled over the soil and pressed in. They germinate in about ten days. If it is necessary to transplant the seedlings, it should be done while they are still small, for mature plants do not transplant well. The young plants should be thinned to six inches apart so that they can reach their full height of a foot and a half. Full sun and average soil are the conditions that summer savory likes. If summer finds the plants too tall and spindly, trim the tips back a few inches to encourage them to branch out. In the fall, savory will scatter its seed freely to give you a new crop the next spring.

Indoors, summer savory will do well with the same general conditions that suit other herbs. Give it plenty of sun and perhaps a bit of lime in its soil. Water whenever the soil feels dry. Keep your plants trimmed back to about eight inches high or you will find that they have a tendency to sprawl.

For centuries savory and beans have been linked together. Savory goes so well with green beans—and all bean dishes—that in many countries it is known as "the bean herb." For instance, in Switzerland it is called *Bohnenkraut*. Herbalists recommended that it be used to reduce the natural "windiness" of beans. However, savory has many other uses. It is one of the great blending herbs and goes well with almost everything. Savory is used with meats, fish, poultry, salads, stuffings, sauces, soups, gravies, meatloaf, and egg dishes. It makes a nice tea, and one of these days you might try throwing a few leaves into your bath water for the sake of its spicy fragrance.

SWEET CICELY
Myrrhis odorata

Sweet cicely deserves a place in this book because it is one of the easiest herbs to grow. It is a very attractive plant too, resembling an enlarged version of chervil with its lacy leaves. Every part of the plant has a sweet licorice taste. Sweet cicely was very popular in Elizabethan times, although its use goes back much farther. It was eaten in salads, used to flavor liqueurs, and given to cows to increase their milk production.

Sweet cicely is a perennial that grows up to three feet tall. It is one of the first plants up in the spring, and one of the first to bloom. The flowers are white and lacy and very pretty. In the fall, sweet cicely is one of the last plants to succumb to frost. The jet black seeds of sweet cicely take months to germinate, so they should be planted in August or September, as soon as they are ripe. The seeds will stay dormant during the winter and sprout in the spring. The new seedlings should be transplanted to two feet apart. Do not try to move them when they are older—year old plants have a tap root up to two inches thick that goes a foot deep. Sweet cicely likes a soil rich in humus. It is one of the few herbs that prefers shade to sun. For this reason, it does well as a foundation planting on the north side of a house. It can also be grown indoors in a shady window if planted in a roomy pot while still small.

The leaves of sweet cicely are useful in salads and as a garnish. The roots were once boiled and eaten as a vegetable. Sweet cicely can be used like tarragon to help reduce the fishy taste of seafood. The unripe seeds are a treat for children, who chew them like licorice candy.

TARRAGON
Artemesia dracunculus

Tarragon is one of the basic and indispensable herbs in French cookery. The dried leaves have a pleasant anise-licorice smell. Chew a pinch of the dried leaves and after a moment, the anise taste will disappear, to be followed by a warm numbing sensation. Arab physicians once took advantage of this by giving their patients a leaf of tarragon to chew so that their tongues would be too numb to taste a dose of bitter medicine.

According to Pliny, tarragon prevented fatigue. In the Middle Ages, many pilgrims tucked leaves of tarragon into their sandals to sustain them on the long and foot-wearying journey to the Holy Land. Tarragon was also valued as an antidote to the bites of small dragons. Here is an excellent example of the Doctrine of Signatures. The roots of tarragon are dense and tangled. To the medieval imagination, they resembled nothing so much as the coiling bodies of serpents - or dragons. The name *dracunculus* means "little dragon." The Franch name is "estragon." Any plant that resembles a dragon can be expected to supply a remedy for its bite. By extension, tarragon was also held to be good for the bites of serpents and venomous insects. Tarragon was a favorite of Charlemagne, but it was not until Tudor times that tarragon reached England, where at first it was grown only in the royal gardens. According to English physicians, tarragon benefitted the head, heart, and liver.

Tarragon is an erect bushy plant that grows two or three feet tall. The leaves are smooth, dark green, and narrow, and release a smell of anise when crushed. The tiny flowers are a greenish-white and appear in loose clusters. The roots, as has been mentioned, form a gnarled and twisted clump. Tarragon should have sun for at least half the day. Good drainage is essential for the successful growth of this plant, far more so than for the other herbs. If its roots are allowed to stand in winter, tarragon quickly dies of root rot. Tarragon needs open space. Plants should be spaced two feet apart and the ground under them kept clear of weeds and other debris. Tarragon is hardy down to 10°F, but in colder climate its survival is chancy without special protection. Propagation of tarragon is accomplished in two ways—by root divisions, and by cuttings.

True tarragon does not make viable seed. Seeds of a related plant are sometimes offered in seed catalogues under the name of tarragon, but this plant is useless for culinary purposes. Cuttings of tarragon root very slowly, so root division is the most satisfactory method of getting new plants. Use a spading fork to lift a clump of tarragon in the spring, carefully pull the tangle of roots apart, and replant the pieces, discarding any that look dead or woody. This should be done every third year anyway so that the crowded roots will have more room to grow.

To keep tarragon green and growing indoors requires more care than most herbs, but tarragon's usefulness in the kitchen makes the extra effort worthwhile. Give the plant plenty of direct sun (at least three or four hours daily) and be sure to provide good drainage. Water when the surface of the soil feels dry and do not overwater. Feed about twice a month. The famous tangled roots of tarragon grow rapidly, and you may have to transfer the plant to a larger pot two or three times a year. A pot of tarragon kept indoors will grow to about a foot high.

Tarragon is most appreciated for its ability to reduce the fishy taste in seafoods. The taste of tarragon is distinctive and individual. It does not mix well with other herbs, so tarragon is usually used alone. Tarragon is good in steaks, chops, poultry, salads, soups, vegetables, omelets, and other egg dishes. Tarragon can also be used to flavor fish sauces, tartar sauce, mayonnaise, vinegar, and pickles. An interesting way to keep tarragon is to place some fresh green leaves in a wide mouthed jar and pour over them red vinegar that has been heated almost to the boiling point. The vinegar becomes tarragon vinegar. The pickled leaves can be taken out, rinsed and used as fresh. One excellent use for them is to stuff a plump-breasted chicken with them for Chicken Tarragon. That should be enough to show you why tarragon is so valued among cooks.

THYME
Thymus vulgaris

Thyme is another of the many herbs from around the edges of the Mediterranean. It was once said that it could not grow where the sea breezes did not blow. Its fragrance made it popular as an incense and a strewing herb long before it was used in food. The odor of thyme was supposed to have healing and purifying properties, and it was widely accepted as a fumigant and antiseptic. The Greeks rubbed their bodies with thyme after bathing. To smell of thyme was considered the fashionable thing. The Romans flavored cheeses and liquors with thyme, and drank its tea and slept on thyme-stuffed pillows to drive away melancholy.

During the Middle Ages, thyme was the symbol of courage, energy, and activity. Knights riding off to the Crusades often carried scarves embroidered by their sweethearts with a bee hovering over a spring of thyme.

Thyme was also worn by young girls to encourage their suitors, and a soup made with thyme and beer was said to overcome shyness. Herbalists wrote that thyme cured melancholy, strengthened the lungs, healed coughs, cured gout, banished dullness of sight, kept away nightmares, and warded off colds. The usefulness of thyme for coughs and colds continues to this day, for the essential oil of thyme, Thymol, has anti-bacterial properties and is used in many cough medicines. Thyme is also a proven melancholy-chaser, for it is a stimulant as well.

Thyme is a sturdy low growing perennial. The spreading woody stems bear little grey-green leaves shaped like arrowheads. The little shrub seldom grows taller than eight inches, but the many branches thickly covered with tiny leaves give it a pleasant bushy look. Thyme flowers in early summer. The light pink or lavender blossoms are very attractive to bees, and it is said that where wild thyme grows you can hear a field before you see it from the humming of the bees. Thyme has been grown and valued as a bee herb since classical times. The famous honey of Mt. Hymettus owes part of its flavor to wild thyme.

Thyme adapts to almost any soil, but it prefers a rich limy one. It also likes at least half a day of sun. Thyme can be grown from seed, but the germination time is long (three or four weeks) and the young plants grow very slowly. They should be thinned to stand about eight inches apart. Mature plants will drop their own seeds. A more satisfying way is to divide the roots of a mature plants, to root cuttings, or to let one of the drooping branches take root to form a new plant that can eventually be cut away from the parent. The low growing habit of ordinary thyme is even more pronounced in creeping thyme *Thymus serphyllum*, which comes in many varieties and can be planted to carpet a path or yard, where it will relase a pleasant fragrance when walked on.

Growing thyme indoors is not difficult if it is given plenty of sun and a little extra lime and fertilizer in its soil. Thyme does not like low humidity, and should have a pan of water nearby if the air in your house tends to be on the dry side. Water thyme when the soil surface feels dry, and wash the leaves from time to time. Drooping branches should be trimmed back to keep the plant looking neat.

Thyme is a very useful herb. It has the happy ability to get along well with almost anything. However, it is a strong herb and should be used sparingly. Fresh leaves are good for salads and vinegar. Dried thyme seasons meats, poultry, fish, chowders, soups, sauces, gravies, cheese dishes, and stuffing. Remember that thyme tea is a traditional remedy for melancholy. It's also good for headaches, and it's even said that thyme tea sweetened with honey and with a pinch of salt will cure a hangover. Yes, thyme is a *very* useful herb.

WINTER SAVORY
Satureia montana

Winter savory is a herb related to summer savory. It gets its name from the fact that it is a perennial and lives through the winter. Its flavor is similar to that of summer savory, but stronger. Before the importation of foreign spices, it was the strongest flavor available to the cook.

Winter savory is a plant with slender glossy leaves on woody stems. It is smaller than summer savory, usually fifteen inches or less. Its flowers are pinkish-white and appear in August. Both winter and summer savory are members of the mint family. Winter savory likes full sun and average soil with a little lime. Plants can be grown both from seeds or from cuttings. Cuttings take a couple of months to become well established. Seeds can be sown in the early spring. Germination time is about two weeks. Plants started from seed require two years to reach flowering size. Winter

80

savory should be clipped from time to time to encourage it to put out new leaves. In some herb gardens it is trimmed into a low hedge to edge a border. Winter savory can also be grown indoors, where it is best kept trimmed to a height of about six inches. Give it the same treatment as summer savory.

Winter savory has the same affinity for beans as summer savory. Some gardeners plant it beside their beans so that the savory will have an extra chance to exert its beneficial influence. Winter savory can be used for other foods in the same manner as summer savory, but keep its strength in mind and use it sparingly.

DRYING HERBS

One of the nice things about herbs is that you can pick a few leaves from your plants any time you need them, spring through fall. By drying them, you can continue to enjoy herbs from your garden through the winter. To harvest your herbs at the height of their flavor, wait until the flower buds are just beginning to open. Harvest on a dry morning, after the dew has dried, but before the sun is high in the sky. You can simply pull up or cut down the annuals (leave a few for seed) but take only the top halves of the perennials, so that they can continue to build strength to survive the winter. Remove any dead or wilted leaves. Then rinse the leaves and blot them as dry as possible between paper towels. Separate the herbs into branches and tie each bunch of stalks together. Each bunch then goes into a paper bag, and the mouth of the bag is gathered around the stem ends and fastened with a rubber band. The bag protects the herbs from dust and light while they dry. Hang the herbs in a dry, well ventilated place (an attic is ideal) for a week or two. Listen for a dry rustle from the bags when you shake them. The leaves should be dry enough to crumble at a touch when you take them out of the bags. If the leaves are not absolutely dry, they will become moldy later. If you have any doubts, allow the leaves to dry for another week, or dry them for a few minutes in a warm (less than 100°F) oven. When you are satisfied that the leaves are dry, strip them from the stalks and crumble them through a coarse strainer. They will keep their pungency for a year or more.

Most books about herbs include charts telling what herb to use with what dish, but these do not do the beginner much good because they do not give any idea of how much of the herb to use. This chart was made after consulting several cookbooks to determine typical amounts for various dishes. It's not intended to replace the cookbooks, of course, but to give you a handy guide as to what is reasonable and to serve as a starting point for your own ideas. The quantities are given in teaspoons (except for bay, which is in leaves). The herbs are assumed to be dried, so if you are using fresh herbs, double the suggested amount. These suggestions are calculated on a basis of four servings—a quart of soup, a pound of meat, four chops, a three pound chicken, enough stuffing to stuff it, a dozen biscuits, etc. If the suggestions seem overly cautious or generous to you, do not hesitate to double or halve them. Naturally it's impossible to summarize many dishes in such a limited space, so do not be surprised if your cookbook has different ideas. Use your own judgement in selecting herbs to blend with each other. In a while you should know your own likes and dislikes well enough that you won't need this chart anymore. Good luck!

	Vegetables	Soups & Stews	Meats	Fish	Poultry	Stuffing	Eggs	Macaroni & Rice	Bisquits
BASIL	½	¼	½	¼	¼	½	¼	½	
BAY	1	1	1	1	1		1	1	
CHERVIL	¼	¼	1				¼		
CHIVES	1	¼	1				4		
DILL	½	½	½	⅛	½		½	½	½
MARJORAM	½	½	¼	¼	¼	¼	¼	½	½
MINT	1	1	½	½					
OREGANO	½	¼	½	½			½		1
PARSLEY	1½	1	3	1½	1	2	2	3	2
ROSEMARY	¼	½	½	⅛	¼	⅛	¼	¼	2
SAGE	¼	¼	½	¼	¼	¼			2
SAVORY	¼	¼	¼	⅛	¼	¼	⅛		
TARRAGON	½	1	¼	1	1		½		
THYME	¼	½	¼	½	¼	⅛	¼	¼	¼

OTHER USES FOR HERBS

Our forefathers found an amazing number of uses for the simple herbs they grow in their gardens. Here are a few for you to try.

Herb Teas

Most of the herbs in this book can be used to make refreshing teas. For each cup, put a teaspoonful of dried leaves, or a tablespoon full of chopped fresh leaves into a glass or earthenware pot (metal will alter the taste). Use more leaves if you find you like a stronger tea. Add boiling water and allow the leaves to steep for five to ten minutes. Do not boil the leaves or allow them to stand too long, or you will have a bitter medicine instead of a pleasant drink.

Thyme tea is cheering, mint teas are good for headaches, and peppermint tea settles the stomach. Catnip tea is relaxing. Dill tea is good before bedtime. Bay and marjoram make pleasantly scented teas. Other herbs to try are sage, lemon balm, lovage, rosemary, lavender, and rose and lemon geraniums. Try mixing herbs with each other and with ordinary tea.

Herb Vinegars

An interesting way to add flavor to sauces, dressings, and salads is to make them with herb flavored vinegar. Herb vinegars are easy to make and an endless variety is possible.

Gather about a cup of young leafy tips from your plants just before the herb flowers. Crush them slightly and put them in a wide mouthed quart jar. Bring a little less than a quart of vinegar almost to boiling point, without letting it boil. Pour the hot vinegar over the leaves, leaving about two inches of space at the top. Cap the jar tightly and leave it in a warm place. Give it a shake each day, and taste it after about a week. If it isn't strong enough to suit you, strain out the leaves, add a fresh bunch, and let them marinate for another week. When the vinegar is done, strain out the leaves, filter it through cloth, and pour it into bottles. Add a leaf of the herb to each bottle for decoration and cap tightly.

Four good herbs to start with are basil, burnet, tarragon, and mint. The purple leafed variety of basil makes a very pretty vinegar. Interesting vinegars can also be made from marjoram, dill caraway, lemon balm, borage, chives, fennel, summer savory, and thyme. You can also experiment with cider, white, and red wine vinegars as the basis for your herb vinegars. The combination are endless, and just might drive you into making a salad every day just to try out your new vinegars.

Incense

In ancient times, herbs were often burned as incense. Save the trimmings and dead leaves from your herb garden to throw into the fireplace, or try sprinkling your favorite dried herb over some hot coals or a lighted piece of charcoal.

Liqueurs

Herbs are basic ingredients in many liqueurs. Mint flavors creme de menthe, and anise flavors anisette. Over a hundred herbs and spices go into the making of Chartreuse. To make your own herb liqueurs, simply place some herbs in brandy and let them sit in a cool place for two days. Strain the herbs out and taste. If you think the flavor isn't strong enough, repeat with fresh herbs. A little clear sugar syrup can be added to bring up the flavor. Some herbs to try are tarragon, mint, marjoram, basil, rosemary, chervil, sweet cicely, fennel, and woodruff.

Herb Butters

An interesting way to add the taste of herbs to your food is to make herb butters. Warm a quarter cup of butter and mix in a tablespoonful of chopped fresh herb leaves or a teaspoonful of dried leaves. Herb butters can be used on hot food at the table or to add interest to sandwiches.

Potpourris

In Victorian times, almost every house had an ornate rose jar filled with a scented mixture of rose petals, spices, and herbs. When the lid was lifted, a delightful fragrance dispelled the stuffiness of the room. A typical potpourri contains about a quart of dried rose petals and herb leaves, about two ounces of an odor holding fixative such as orris root or gum benzoin, a couple tablespoonfuls of crushed spices, perhaps a few drops of essential oils, and a little brandy to blend the fragrances and give them carrying power. Making a potpourri takes a lot of time and patience but the result is worthwhile, and a good potpourri lasts for years.

The most difficult part about making a potpourri is gathering and drying enough rose petals. The petals should be gathered when the dew has dried, before the sun is high in the sky. Then they must be spread on a tray in the sun each day, out of the wind, until they are dry. When they are properly dried, the petals will have lost most of their weight but not their color. If you dry them to the point of crispness and browness, they will also lose their odor.

The next step in drying the petals is to place them in a jar with about half a pound of salt. The job of the salt is to absorb any remaining moisture. Uncover the jar and stir daily. It will take a few weeks for the petals to dry completely, so you can use this time to prepare other ingredients. For instance, you can dry the petals of other garden flowers to add color to the mixture. Gather and dry your favorite fragrant herbs, and buy the freshest whole cloves, allspice, and cinnamon you can find.

When the rose petals are completely dry, sift out most of the salt. Mix your herbs, spices, and fixatives, and pound them all together. Add them to the rose petals and put the mixture in a large jar. Now add an ounce of brandy. Keep the mixture covered, but stir it daily to help blend the various scents. After a couple of weeks of this, you can put the potpourri in its display jar. If you want to add a final touch, you can take the jar to your druggist and ask him to add two or three drops of attar of roses or some other essential oil. Your popourri should please you for years.

Sources for Herb Seeds, Plants, and Products

Not all the herbs mentioned in this book are popular enough to be included in common seed catalogues. Below are some mail order sources which offer a wide variety of herbs, including many of the less well-known ones.

Green Herb Garden   seeds
Greene, Rhode Island 02827

Meadowbrook Herb Garden   plants, seeds, herb products
Wyoming, Rhode Island 02898

Merry Gardens   plants
Camden, Maine 04843

Caprilands Herb Farm
Silver St.
Coventry, Conn. 06238

Aphrodisia   herb products
28 Carmine St.
New York, New York 10014

The Tool Shed Herb Nursery   plants
Turkey Hill Rd.
Salem Center
Purdy Station, N.Y. 10578

Rocky Hollow Herb Farm
Lake Wallkill Rd.
Sussex, N.J.

Penn Herb Company   herb products
603 N. 2nd Street
Phila, Pa. 19123

The Herb Cottage   plants
The Washington Cathedral
Mount St. Alban
Washington, D.C. 20016

George Park Seed Company Inc. seeds
Greenwood, S.C. 29646

Pine Hill Herb Farm
Box 307
Roswell, Ga. 30075

Sunnybrook Farms Nursery   plants
9448 Mayfield Rd.
Cherterland, Ohio 44026

Indiana Botanic Gardens, Inc. herb products
Hammond, Indiana 46325

Northwestern Processing Co.   herb products
217 North Broadway
Milwaukee, Wis. 53202

Gurney Seed & Nursery
Yankton, S.D. 57078

Oak Ridge Herb Farm   seeds, plants, herb products
R.R. 1 Box 461
Alton, Ill. 62002

Hilltop Herb Farm   plants
Box 866
Cleveland, Texas 77327

Herb Products Company   herb products
11012 Magnolia Blvd.
North Hollywood, Calif. 91601

Taylor's Garden
2649 Stringle Avenue
Rosemead, Cal. 91770

Vita Green Farms   seeds
P.O. Box 878
Vista, Calif. 92083

Snow Line Herb Farm
11846 Fremont Street
Yucaipa, Calif. 92399

W. Atlee Burpee Company
P.O. Box 748
Riverside, Calif. 92502
or   seeds
P.O. Box 6929
Phila, Pa. 19132

Mail Box Seeds   seeds
Shirley Morgan
2042 Encinal Ave.
Alameda, Calif. 94501

Lhasa Kharnak Herb Co.   herb products
2482 Telegraph Ave.
Berkeley, Calif. 94704

Nature's Herb Co.   herb products
281 Ellis St.
San Francisco, Calif.

Nichol's Garden Nursery   seeds, plants, herb products
1190 North Pacific Hwy.
Albany, Oregon 97321

Waynefield Herbs
837 Cosgrove St.
Port Townsend, Wash. 98368

World-Wide Herbs, Ltd.   seeds, herb products
11 St. Catherine St. East
Montreal 129, Canada

Dominion Herb Distribution Inc.   seeds, herb produts
61 St. Catherine St. West
Montreal 129, Quebec, Canada

Otto Richter & Sons Ltd.
Locust Hill,
Ontario, Canada

Many more herb sources are listed in the Herb Buyer's Guide, a ten cent booklet published by:

The Herb Society of America
300 Massachusetts Avenue
Boston, Mass. 02115